PRELUDE TO A KISS

Craig Lucas

357 W 20th St, NY NY 10011
212 627-1055

PRELUDE TO A KISS
Copyright © 1990 by Craig Lucas

First printing: August 1990
Second printing: August 1992
ISBN: 0-88145-067-7

Book design: Marie Donovan
Word processing: WordMarc Composer Plus
Typographic controls: Xerox Ventura Publisher,
Professional Extension
Typeface: Palatino
Printed on acid-free paper and bound in the USA.

ABOUT THE AUTHOR

Craig Lucas is the author of MISSING PERSONS, RECKLESS, and BLUE WINDOW. With composer/lyricist Craig Carnelia he wrote the musical play THREE POSTCARDS. With his frequent collaborator, director Norman René, he conceived and developed MARRY ME A LITTLE, an evening of songs by Stephen Sondheim. He has written the screenplays for BLUE WINDOW and LONGTIME COMPANION, both produced by American Playhouse and directed by Mr René. He has received the George and Elisabeth Marton Award, the L.A. Drama Critics' Award, three Drama-Logue Awards, Guggenheim and Rockefeller grants, two Drama Desk nominations for Best Play, and an Obie Award. THREE POSTCARDS was selected as Best Musical of 1986-87 by the Burns Mantle Theater Yearbook. LONGTIME COMPANION received the Audience Award for Best Dramatic Film at the 1990 Sundance U.S. Film Festival. He is a member of the Dramatists Guild.

PRELUDE TO A KISS was commissioned by South Coast Repertory, where it premiered on 15 January 1988. The cast and creative contributors were as follows:

*GINNY	Roberta Farkas
PETER	Mark Arnott
TAYLOR	Michael Canavan
RITA	Lisa Zane
*NANCY	Anni Long
TOM	Art Koustik
MRS BOYLE	Teri Ralston
DR BOYLE	Hal Landon, Jr.
MINISTER	John-David Keller
AUNT DOROTHY	Roberta Farkas
*FAMILY FRIEND	Anni Long
*FAMILY FRIEND'S HUSBAND	Don Took
OLD MAN	Frank Hamilton
LEAH	Mary Anne McGarry
ENSEMBLE	Lisa Black, Cynthia Blaise, Edgar W. Chambers, Patrick Massoth, Roberta Ornellas, Paul J. Read, Catherine Rowe

*(*Roles cut from present version)*

Director	Norman René
Sets	Loy Arcenas
Costumes	Walker Hicklin
Lighting	Peter Maradudin
Sound design	Serge Ossorguine
Stage manager	Julie Haber
Dramaturg	John Glore

A revised version premiered at Circle Repertory
Company on 14 March 1990. The cast and creative
contributors were as follows:

PETER .... Alec Baldwin
TAYLOR .... John Dossett
RITA .... Mary-Louise Parker
TOM .... L Peter Callender
MRS BOYLE .... Debra Monk
DR BOYLE .... Larry Bryggman
MINISTER .... Craig Bockhorn
AUNT DOROTHY .... Joyce Reehling
UNCLE FRED .... Michael Warren Powell
OLD MAN .... Barnard Hughes
JAMAICAN WAITER .... L Peter Callender
LEAH .... Joyce Reehling
ENSEMBLE .... Kimberly Dudwitt, Pete Tyler

Director .... Norman René
Sets .... Loy Arcenas
Costumes .... Walker Hicklin
Lighting .... Debra J Kletter
Sound design .... Scott Lehrer
Hair and wig design .... Bobby H Grayson
Stage manager .... M.A. Howard

PRELUDE TO A KISS then moved to Broadway, at the Helen Hayes Theatre, opening on 1 May 1990. It was produced by Christopher Gould, Suzanne Golden, and Dodger Productions. The cast and creative contributors remained the same, with the following changes:

PETER .... Timothy Hutton
ENSEMBLE .... Brian Cousins

Production stage manager ....James Harker

CHARACTERS
(in order of speaking)

PETER
TAYLOR
RITA
TOM
MRS BOYLE
DR BOYLE
MINISTER
AUNT DOROTHY
UNCLE FRED
OLD MAN
JAMAICAN WAITER
LEAH

Party guests, barflies, wedding guests, vacationers

PLAYWRIGHT'S NOTE

To provide a fluidity of motion and to stress the imaginary leap required to make sense of the story, PRELUDE was originally staged with a minimum of scenery — a chair and lamp to indicate RITA's apartment, a free-standing bar for The Tin Market, a pair of chaise lounges for Jamaica — allowing the lighting to do the bulk of the work in transforming the space. We also used a great deal of underscoring with source music and sound effects (surf, traffic, popular songs, marimba bands in Jamaica), again to indicate place and create a kind of magic. PETER often changed clothes in front of our eyes, and the scenery came to him on tracks, gliding quietly. Upstage, a permanent green wall, as if in a garden, suggested that things were more than they might seem; in that wall was a large window looking out on a changing sky — night stars, distorted sunsets for Jamaica — and a twisted vine climbed up alongside the window frame. If lit from the front, the sky behind the window disappeared and a greenish, painted sky of clouds made the window once again part of the wall itself.

I would like to thank all of my collaborators in the various productions and readings of the play — the director, dramaturgs, designers, and actors. In addition, I am grateful to the Guggenheim Foundation for their generous support during rewrites, and to Kip Gould for providing enhancement money at Circle Rep.

Then the King's daughter began to weep and was afraid of the cold frog, whom nothing would satisfy but he must sleep in her pretty clean bed.

—Brothers Grimm, *The Frog Prince*

Death destroys a man, but the idea of death is what saves him.

—E.M. Forster, *Howards End*

ACT ONE

(Music. We hear a recorded vocalist as the lights go down: "If you hear a song in blue,/Like a flower crying for the dew,/ That was my heart serenading you,/My prelude to a kiss.")

(A crowded party. PETER *stands apart, then approaches* TAYLOR.*)*

PETER: I'm splitting.... Hey, Tay?

TAYLOR: Hey, Pete, did you meet Rita?

PETER: No. Hi.

RITA: Hi.

TAYLOR: *(Overlapping)* Rita, Peter, Peter, Rita.

PETER: Actually, I...

TAYLOR: *(Overlapping)* What's everybody drinking? Reet? Can I fill you up there?

RITA: Oh, I'll have another Dewar's, thanks.

TAYLOR: Pete?

PETER: No, nothing, thank —

TAYLOR: Don't worry, I've got it taken care of. You two just relax. One Dewar's, one beer...

(He moves off. Pause.)

PETER: How do you know the Sokols?

RITA: I don't. I mean, except from the hall.

PETER: Oh, you're a neighbor.

RITA: I couldn't sleep.

PETER: Oh, really? Why?... How long have you lived here?

RITA: I haven't slept since I was fourteen. A year and a half.

(Beat)

PETER: Did you say you hadn't slept since you were fourteen?

RITA: Pretty much.

PETER: You look great!

RITA: Thank you.

PETER: Considering. Rita what?

RITA: Boyle.

PETER: Peter Hoskins.

RITA: Hoskins?

PETER: As in Hoskins disease?

RITA: Oh, Hodgkins.

PETER: No, no, it was just a...nonhumorous...flail.

RITA: What? *(He shakes his head.)* I like your shirt!

(TAYLOR returns with drinks.)

TAYLOR: Dewar's, Madame?

RITA: Thank you.

TAYLOR: No beer, sorry.

PETER: Wine's fine. Thanks... Rita has insomnia.

TAYLOR: Oh yeah? Listen, I've got to pee, I'm sorry, excuse me. Forgive me...

(He is gone again.)

PETER: What do you do when you're not NOT sleeping?

RITA: Oh, I usually, you know...write in my journal or —... Oh, for a living, you mean? I'm a bartender.

PETER: Oh. Where?

RITA: *(Overlapping)* Yeah. At the Tin Market.

PETER: Oh, I know where that is. One for Pete.

RITA: Yeah.

PETER: I guess it's a good place for an insomniac to work. You work Saturdays? *(She nods.)* Well, you must make good money. Well, so you hate it, I'm sorry, I can't help that. What are your aspirations, in that case?

RITA: I'm like a graphic designer.

PETER: Oh, great.

RITA: I studied at Parsons.

PETER: This is good.

RITA: What do you do?

PETER: I make little tiny, transparent photographs of scientific articles which are rolled on film like microfilm only smaller. You'd like it. It's really interesting.

RITA: What are your aspirations in that case?

PETER: I should have some, shouldn't I? No, I I I I I I, uh, can't think of the answer, I'm sorry.

RITA: That's okay!

PETER: So why can't you sleep? You know what's good? I forget what it's called, it's an herb.

RITA: I tried it.

PETER: It didn't work?

RITA: I can't remember what it's called either. My memory is terrible!

PETER: Maybe that's why you can't sleep. You forget how tired you are. Well... If you ever need any help getting to sleep. *(Beat)* Sorry. *(Beat)* It was nice talking to you.

RITA: You, too.

PETER: Get some sleep.

RITA: I'll try.

(PETER addresses the audience)

PETER: I stood outside for a while, just listening to the silence. Then I tried to figure out which window was hers and what her life might be like and why she couldn't sleep. Like that. *(Beat)* The spell was cast.

(The Tin Market)

PETER: Hi.

RITA: Oh, hi.

PETER: Is this all right?

RITA: No, I'm sorry, you can never come in here.... What's new?

PETER: Since yesterday? Well, let's see, so much has happened. You look great.

RITA: What'll you drink?

PETER: Do you have Molson?... *(She nods.)* So, did you get some sleep?

RITA: Eventually.

(She sets down his Molson.)

PETER: Thank you.

RITA: You?

PETER: Sleep? Oh, I don't have any trouble. But...let's see, I read *The White Hotel* today.

RITA: Oh.

PETER: That was pretty much it.

RITA: Yeah.

PETER: You?

RITA: Oh, I slept, mostly.... How was *The White Hotel*?

PETER: Did you read it?

RITA: No, but I've read some of the case histories it's based on.

PETER: You have? Freud's? Case histories? You've read Freud.

RITA: Have you?

PETER: No, but... This book?

RITA: Uh-huh?

PETER: Starts with this very high-falutin' sexual dream thing, you know?

RITA: Yeah, I've heard everybody beats off when they read it.

(Beat)

PETER: Uh-huh.

RITA: I'm sorry.

PETER: You heard that?

RITA: Go on.

PETER: ...It's very depressing, the book.

RITA: Uh-huh.

PETER: This lovely, very neurotic woman goes into therapy with Freud himself —

RITA: Right.

PETER: And he sort of cures her so that she can go on to live for a few years before being killed by the Nazis in a lime pit. Happy. Happy stuff.

RITA: So why were you in Europe for ten years?

PETER: How did you know I was in Europe?

RITA: Word gets around.

PETER: You asked Taylor about me? You were asking around about me? Let's get married.

RITA: Okay.

PETER: I just went, you know.

RITA: He said there was a story and you would have to tell me.

PETER: He did?... Okay, this is the story and I'm not making this up.

RITA: Okay.

PETER: And it's not as sad as it sounds.

RITA: Shoot.

PETER: My parents?

RITA: Uh-huh?

PETER: Separated when I was four. And I went to live with my grandparents who are unfortunately deceased now. I'm going to make this as brief as possible.

RITA: Take your time.

PETER: And —

RITA: We can go up to my place if you want. When you're done.

PETER: And-everything-worked-out-great-for-everybody-it-was-amazing.

RITA: No, go on.

PETER: Were you serious about that?

RITA: I'm off in about seven minutes. Your parents.

PETER: My parents. I'm four years old. I go to live with my grandparents. My grandfather had to go into a nursing home when I was nine, then my grandmother had to go when I was eleven; they were both sick, so I go to live with my mother who by this time is remarried to Hank.

RITA: Uh-huh.

PETER: Very unhappy person, ridicules me in front of the other two children they have created from their unsavory loins, so I go to live with my father, who is also remarried, *three* other children, Sophie, the new wife, hates me even more than Hank.

RITA: This is like Dickens.

PETER: The only nice thing Sophie ever did for me was make the same food twice when I had made the mistake of saying I liked it. Usually she would stop cooking whatever it was I said I liked.

RITA: What was it?

PETER: What I liked? Spaetzles?

RITA: Oh, god.

PETER: You've had spaetzles?

RITA: Oh, sure.

PETER: You like them?

RITA: I love them.

PETER: You do?

RITA: Uh-huh. Anyway.

PETER: You love spaetzles. Anyway, everyone is unhappy now.

RITA: Uh-huh.

PETER: Sophie really can't stand the sight of me, because I remind her that my father was married to someone else and....

RITA: Right.

PETER: And my father does not seem too fond of me, either. I don't know if he ever was, but so one night I say I'm going to go to the movies and instead I go to Europe.

RITA: What movie?

PETER: *The Wild Bunch,* I think, why?

RITA: Did you call them first?

PETER: Not until I got there.

RITA: Europe?

PETER: And I called collect.

RITA: That is....

PETER: Yeah.

RITA: Good for you.

PETER: Yeah. So. Why'd you ask which movie?

RITA: That is fabulous.

PETER: That's the story.

RITA: How did you eat? I mean....

PETER: Oh, I had about three thousand dollars saved up from my paper route. But that's a whole other kettle of....

RITA: Spaetzles.

PETER: Yeah. So...

RITA: You lived in Amsterdam?

PETER: You're a spy, aren't you?

(TOM *enters, behind the bar.*)

TOM: Hey, kiddo.

RITA: Hi. Tom, this is Peter.

TOM: Hi.

PETER: Good to meet you.

RITA: *(To* PETER*)* You want to go?

PETER: Now? Naaaaaaaa. *(To us)* I love the little sign when you buy your ticket to the roller coaster: "Ride at your own risk." As if the management is not at all concerned with your safety, the entire contraption is about to collapse, and to top it off, there are supernatural powers out there just waiting to pull you off the tracks and out into, you know, your worst, cruelest nightmare — the wild blue. They want you to believe that anything can happen. *(Beat)* And they're right.

(Outside. They walk.)

PETER: Uh-huh.

RITA: So.

PETER: So they disowned you?

RITA: No. I never told them.

PETER: Oh.

RITA: It was like...I mean, they didn't need to know what I was involved with. I don't tell them everything.

PETER: I've never known a Communist.

RITA: Socialist.

PETER: Socialist.

RITA: But...I mean, I was only in the Party for about two months.

PETER: What happened?

RITA: Oh, I just...I felt like they were basically not interested in anything except being right.

PETER: Right.

RITA: And they didn't support the Soviet Union, not that they should —

PETER: Uh-huh.

RITA: —and they didn't support Mao, and they didn't support the United States. It's like where are you going to live?

PETER: Right.

RITA: But...I started by doing leaflets for them and then posters. I still did that after I left. What?

PETER: Nothing.

RITA: It was such a strange time.... You're a good listener.

PETER: So now you're....

RITA: Oh, I guess I'm a Democrat.

PETER: Me too.

RITA: But...they're such Republicans.

PETER: Your parents?

RITA: No, the Democrats. Beneath the skin.

PETER: Oh, uh-huh?

RITA: But...I don't know. I guess it's like the U.S. It isn't perfect.

PETER: Right. *(Pause)* Where do they live?

RITA: My parents? Englewood Cliffs. It's right across the bridge. It's nice, actually.

PETER: What do they do?

RITA: My dad's a dentist.

PETER: Oh, really?

RITA: Uh-huh.

PETER: Wow.

RITA: Why?

PETER: No, I just think that's...interesting.

RITA: It is?

PETER: I think so. I don't know.

RITA: My mother's a mother.

PETER: Do you have brothers and sisters? *(She shakes her head.)* They must dote on you.

RITA: What's Amsterdam like? D'you speak Dutch?

PETER: Ja.

RITA: Say something in Dutch.

PETER: Uh... Je hebt erg witte tanden.

RITA: What's that?

PETER: You have very white teeth.

RITA: Oh. Thank you.

PETER: Now you say, Om je better mee op te eten.

RITA: What is it?

PETER: Om je better mee op te eten.

RITA: Om je metter—

PETER: Better...

RITA: Better...

PETER: ...mee op te eten.

RITA: ...mee op te eten.

PETER: Om je better mee op te eten.

RITA: Om je better mee op te eten.

PETER: Great. You've got a good ear.

RITA: Oh. Good ear, clean teeth.

PETER: You do.

RITA: What did I say?

PETER: I can't tell you.

RITA: *(Overlapping)* I knew you were gonna say that, I knew it!

PETER: No, it's untranslatable.

RITA: I'm sure it is. No, come on.

PETER: I'll tell you someday....

RITA: So what did you do there?

PETER: In Amsterdam? I will, I promise.

RITA: How old were you when you went?

PETER: Sixteen.

RITA: Oh, wow.

PETER: I catered for the first couple of years and made sandwiches during the day; then I tutored rich little cutie-pies on their English and went to school at night. Finally I came back when my dad died.

(Pause)

RITA: Do you see your mom or your family at all? *(He shakes his head.)* Never?

PETER: Nope.

RITA: Do you call them? *(He shakes his head.)* You miss them?

(Headshake. Pause.)

(RITA's apartment)

PETER: This is great.

RITA: You want a Molson?

PETER: You drink Molson—

RITA: Uh-huh.

PETER: —in your own home?

RITA: I've been known to.

PETER: That's really....

RITA: A coincidence.

PETER: A coincidence. So why can't you sleep? I want to solve this.

RITA: I really wasn't exaggerating. It's been since I was fourteen.

PETER: That's a lot of journal keeping.... Have you seen doctors?

RITA: I've seen all the doctors.

PETER: Uh-huh.

RITA: Of every known...

PETER: Right.

RITA: *(Overlapping)* Persuasion. I've ingested countless...

(She hands him a Molson.)

PETER: Thanks.

RITA: Pills, liquids, I've seen an acupuncturist.

PETER: You did? What did it feel like?

RITA: Little needles in your back.

PETER: It hurt?

RITA: Sometimes.

PETER: They always lie.

RITA: I know.

PETER: You're really beautiful. *(She laughs.)* You are.

RITA: Thank you. That's.... No, thank you.

(They kiss. She laughs.)

PETER: This is not supposed to be the funny part.

RITA: No, I know, I'm sorry.... I'm, I guess I'm nervous.

PETER: Why are you nervous? Don't be nervous.

RITA: All right.

(He approaches to kiss her.)

PETER: Don't laugh... All right, you can laugh. *(They kiss.)* Am I going too fast? *(She shakes her head.)* Is this tacky of me? *(Headshake)* Oh good. *(They kiss.)* This is definitely the highlight of my weekend. *(She smiles.)* So maybe we should just, you know, watch some TV, have happy memories of this and anticipate the future — *(She is shaking her head.)* —We shouldn't? *(They kiss.)* I would really, really like to see you with all of your clothes off and stuff like that.

RITA: I would really, really like to see you with all of your clothes off and....

PETER: Stuff like that? *(To us)* When you're first getting to know someone and in that blissful, psychotic first flush of love, it seems like every aspect of their personality, their whole demeanor, the simple, lovely twist of their earlobes and their marvelous phone voice and their soft, dark wet whatever is somehow imbued

with an extra push of color, an intensity heretofore...
you know. *Unknown.*

(RITA's *apartment. Later.*)

PETER: Christ!

RITA: What?

PETER: Happiness!... Are you?

RITA: Uh-huh.

PETER: You are? It's like a drug.

RITA: It is a drug.

PETER: Sex?

RITA: To snare us into mating.

PETER: I must be peaking then.

RITA: No, the body manufactures it.

PETER: Uh-huh.

RITA: Like epinephrine or something.

PETER: Maybe that's where they got the word "crack".

RITA: Shut up. I prefer hole. Frankly.

PETER: Hole?

RITA: And dick.

PETER: Slit.

RITA: Ugh.

PETER: This is sick.

RITA: Tool, I like.

PETER: Uh-huh.

RITA: It's practical.

PETER: Wait a minute, did I detect an earlier note of cynicism in your comment about mating?

RITA: Oh. No.

PETER: You don't like kids?

RITA: No, I love them.

PETER: But you don't want to have them?

RITA: No, I don't, but....

PETER: Why not?

RITA: I just don't.

PETER: Your career?

RITA: What career? No, I think kids are great, I just don't think it's fair to raise them in the world. The way it is now.

PETER: Where else are you going to raise them? We're here.

RITA: I know, but....

PETER: It's like what you were saying about the socialists. (RITA *hesitates.*) Say.

RITA: Like...the woman in *The White Hotel.* People really do struggle their whole lives just to die in lime pits, and not just in books. Women go blind from watching their children being murdered.

PETER: Not in this country they don't.

RITA: No, they get shot on the sidewalk in front of their houses in some drug war. I mean, just what you went through being passed from one parent to another who didn't even—

PETER: I survived....

(Pause)

RITA: I'll be lying in bed late at night and I'll look at the light in the room and suddenly see it all just go up in a blinding flash, in flames, and I'm the only one left alive.... I can't look at you sitting there without imagining you...dying...bursting into flames....

PETER: No wonder you can't sleep.

RITA: The world's a really terrible place. It's too precarious. *(Pause)* You want kids, obviously. I wish I could say I did.

PETER: It's okay.

RITA: What's your dirtiest fantasy?

PETER: Excuse me? No, I thought you just said what's my dirtiest fantasy.

RITA: What?

PETER: No, I can't—

RITA: Yes, you can. Please?

PETER: I'm sorry, I can't. What's yours, though? I'd be curious.

RITA: *(Overlapping)* I asked you first. Come on.

PETER: Oh god.

RITA: Please.

PETER: Well, they change.

RITA: Sure. What's one?

PETER: One?

RITA: Uh-huh.

PETER: Well... One?

RITA: Uh-huh.

PETER: Might be that someone...you know....

RITA: Uh-huh.

PETER: —who might just happen to be around the apartment—

RITA: Uh-huh.

PETER: *(Mimicking her)* Uh-huh, uh-huh. Might...sort of just, you know, spontaneously start crawling across the floor—

RITA: Uh-huh.

PETER: —on their hands and knees and...more or less unzip me with their, uh...teeth.

RITA: I'd do that.

PETER: You would?

RITA: Uh-huh.

PETER: Right now? *(She nods; to us:)* We saw each other every night for the next six weeks. And it wasn't just the knees and the teeth, despite what you think. I would stop by my apartment now and then to see if the view out onto the airshaft had improved any, but my clothes had all found their way over to Rita's and my books. And then...

(RITA's apartment. Six weeks later. PETER is serving dinner.)

PETER: That was the Communist?

RITA: Socialist.

PETER: Socialist.

RITA: No. That was the one who liked to dress up, go out.

PETER: Oh, right. But you don't like to go dancing, do you?

RITA: Sometimes. I change.

PETER: Uh-huh.

RITA: People do.

PETER: So before that was the Communist?

RITA: Socialist.

PETER: *(Overlapping)* Socialist. And before that...?

RITA: Oh, it was just high school, you know. This looks great. No, wait, there was someone else, who was it?

PETER: Is that what's going to happen to me?

RITA: Oh no, John, I told you about John.

PETER: The one who wanted to run away with you? Is that what's going to happen to me?

RITA: You're gonna want to run away?

PETER: You're going to forget my name over dinner with someone else equally enamored of you and just attribute it to your lousy memory? "Oh, yes, that's right, Peter. Peter—"

RITA: Probably.

PETER: "What did he look like?" And then you'll tell them my dirtiest fantasy and how you degraded yourself just for a home-cooked meal.

RITA: Mmmm. *(They are eating.)* I told my parents about you.

PETER: What did you tell them?

RITA: I said that you were very considerate.

PETER: In what way?

RITA: I said— Well, I mean, we talk very frankly about sex.

PETER: You and your parents?

RITA: And I said that you always brought protection....

PETER: You did not.

RITA: And that you were very attentive to whether or not I had an orgasm.

PETER: This is such bullshit.

RITA: No, I said they should meet you, what do you think?

PETER: Protection.

RITA: They're nice.

PETER: I'm sure.

RITA: So are you free this weekend?

PETER: Sure.

RITA: Don't be nervous.

PETER: All right. Did you tell them about my family and everything?

RITA: My mother.

PETER: She knows the story?

RITA: Uh-huh.

PETER: All about me?

RITA: Uh-huh.

PETER: Will you marry me?

RITA: Uh-huh.

PETER: You will?

RITA: Uh-huh.

(Beat)

PETER: I just wanted to see how it sounds.

RITA: It sounds great.

PETER: This is too fast. Isn't it?

RITA: Is it?

PETER: I don't think so.

RITA: Neither do I.

PETER: You'll marry me?

RITA: Uh-huh.

PETER: You will?

RITA: Uh-huh.

(The BOYLE *home. Doorbell.)*

RITA: Mom?

MRS BOYLE: Nice to meet you.

RITA: Dad.

PETER: Dr. Boyle.

RITA: These are my parents....

MRS BOYLE: So I understand you're a manager in a publishing firm.

PETER: That's correct. Yes.

DR BOYLE: That must be, uh.... What kind of firm is it?

MRS BOYLE: Publishing.

DR BOYLE: What kind — Don't belittle me in front of new people.

MRS BOYLE: Belittle?

RITA: Dad, please.

DR BOYLE: What kind of publishing firm is it? I was asking.

PETER: It's, uh, scientific publishing. They publish, you know, scientific publishing — things — journals! I knew I knew that.

RITA: *(To* PETER*)* You want a beer?

PETER: Sure.

MRS BOYLE: In the morning, Rita?

RITA: Yes, Mother, we have been drinking nonstop for weeks, it's time you knew this about us.

MRS BOYLE: I'll have one too, then.

RITA: You will?

DR BOYLE: Me, too.

PETER: A bunch of lushes here, Rita, you didn't tell me.

DR BOYLE: Oh, I can pull out four wisdom teeth on a fifth of Stoli.

PETER: You can?

MRS BOYLE: He's teasing you.

DR BOYLE: Scien— What kind of scientific?

PETER: Abstracting and indexing. It's a service.

DR BOYLE: Like a database.

PETER: It is a database.

DR BOYLE: It is a database. Covering...?

PETER: All kinds of fields.

DR BOYLE: All kinds.

PETER: Pretty much, you know, everything from energy to robotics to medical articles. I've memorized our marketing material.

DR BOYLE: I've seen this.

(RITA *hands everyone his/her beer.*)

PETER: Thank you.

(*They clink bottles.*)

DR BOYLE: I've seen this sort of thing.

PETER: Yeah.

DR BOYLE: So you're the manager...?

PETER: The manager of the fiche department.

DR BOYLE: Microfiche.

PETER: Right.

MRS BOYLE: The what is it?

DR BOYLE: Microfiche.

PETER: It's like microfilm only smaller.

MRS BOYLE: Uh-huh.

PETER: Little film.

DR BOYLE: Why do you do that?

PETER: Microfiche?

DR BOYLE: No, why does the company do microfiche?

PETER: Oh, I see. Because if you want to call up and —

DR BOYLE: Oh, I — yes, yes, yes, yes, yes.

PETER: *(Overlapping)* — ask for like —

DR BOYLE: Right, a certain article.

PETER: Right. We can retrieve it for you. And we also film the abstract journals we actually publish so....

DR BOYLE: To save space.

PETER: Right. Yes, in libraries, it saves space.

DR BOYLE: All right. We approve.

RITA: Daddy.

MRS BOYLE: Marshall.

DR BOYLE: Maybe now she'll get some sleep.

MRS BOYLE: Now how long have you two been going out?

RITA: Over a year now.

(PETER *looks at* RITA; *beat.*)

PETER: About that. Yeah.

MRS BOYLE: Rita says you've been abroad.

PETER: Yes, I have.

MRS BOYLE: Where?

PETER: Amsterdam, for the most part, but...

MRS BOYLE: Marshall was in Korea.

PETER: Oh, was it nice? Oh, no, no, I see —

MRS BOYLE: Nice!

DR BOYLE: Some people might have been able to relax, I don't know, bullets flying.

PETER: *(Overlapping)* Right. Right.

MRS BOYLE: We're playing with you.

DR BOYLE: Okay, here you go.

(DR BOYLE *starts to untuck his shirttail.*)

RITA: Oh no, Daddy, please, god, please —

DR BOYLE: *(Overlapping)* This is the only scar you'll ever see in the shape of a saxophone.

MRS BOYLE: It really is, people think he's kidding.

PETER: Really?

DR BOYLE: If he's going to be in the family, he's got to see these things.

(*The* BOYLE *home. A month later.*)

PETER: *(To us, as he changes into his wedding garb)* I stood in front of the full-length mirror in their upstairs guestroom, looking out over the yard at the little tent and the band and the food which had been catered; I felt a certain kinship with these people, the caterers.

(RITA *sneaks up, covers his eyes.*)

RITA: Don't look, it's bad luck.

PETER: All right, but— Wait, wait— You don't believe that, do you?

RITA: *(Overlapping)* You looked.

PETER: I didn't look.

RITA: You're looking.

PETER: Wait, I won't look. I won't.

RITA: *(Overlapping)* No, you've already cursed the first fourteen years of our marriage.

PETER: I love you.

RITA: What about when I'm a hundred years old with a moustache and yellow teeth?

PETER: I'll still love you.

RITA: And I'm sagging down to here and I'm bald?

PETER: I'll love you all the more.

RITA: Are you sure?

PETER: Yes, I promise.

RITA: And I won't ever want to make love and I can never remember anything?

PETER: You can never remember anything now.

RITA: That's true. Okay.

(*She leaves;* PETER'*s eyes remain closed.*)

PETER: What about me?

(TAYLOR *comes in with two beers; he is wearing sunglasses.*)

TAYLOR: What about you?... You okay?

PETER: Great, Taylor.

TAYLOR: They're holding for the musicians.

PETER: Okay.

(TAYLOR *helps* PETER *dress.*)

TAYLOR: Now listen. There's nothing at all to worry about here.

PETER: I know that.

TAYLOR: This is a natural step in life's plan. Like sliding down a bannister.

PETER: Right.

TAYLOR: That turns into a razor blade. No, I don't want you to think of this as anything more than one of the little skirmishes we all wage, each and every day of our lives, in the eternal struggle against mediocrity and decay. Straighten your tie.

PETER: I straightened my tie.

TAYLOR: Fix your face. You're not compromising yourself.

PETER: Thank you.

TAYLOR: Not at all. You see all those middle-aged guys down there in their checked pants and their wives in the flouncy dresses?

PETER: Mm-hm.

TAYLOR: They were all very hip once. But... There's the music. You okay?

PETER: Just go.

TAYLOR: Relax. I've got the ring.

PETER: Great. Go.

(TAYLOR *kisses* PETER *on the cheek, mouths "I love you".*)

(The BOYLE *home. Outside.)*

MINISTER: ...to keep the solemn vows you are about to make. Live with tender consideration for each other. Conduct your lives in honesty and in truth. And your marriage will last. This should be remembered as you now declare your desire to be wed.

PETER: I, Peter, take thee, Rita, to be my wedded wife, to have and to hold from this day forward, for better or for worse, for richer or for poorer, in sickness and in health, to love and to cherish, till death us do part, according to God's holy ordinance; and thereto, I pledge thee my troth.

RITA: I, Rita, take thee, Peter, to be my wedded husband, to have and to hold from this day forward, for better or for worse, for richer or for poorer, *(Halting)* in sickness and in health, to love and to cherish, till death us do part, according to God's holy ordinance; and thereto, I pledge thee my troth.

MINISTER: For as much as Rita and Peter have consented together in holy matrimony and have witnessed the same before God and this company, pledging their faith and declaring the same, I pronounce, by the authority committed unto me as a Minister of God, that they are Husband and Wife, according to the ordinance of God and the law of this State, in the Name of the Father, and of the Son, and of the Holy Spirit.... *(*PETER *and* RITA *kiss.)* I think a little applause would be in order.

PETER: *(To us)* And there was some polite applause as if we'd made a good putt or something, and we all made a beeline for the champagne with the strawberries in it.

(The BOYLE *home; outside. Later.)*

~~RITA: Peter, you remember my Aunt Dorothy and Uncle Fred.~~

~~PETER: Yes, good to see you~~.

UNCLE FRED: Peter and Rita, that's very euphonious.

PETER: Yes.

AUNT DOROTHY: Isn't it?

RITA: Sometimes we get Peter and Reeter.

AUNT DOROTHY: Oh.

RITA: Or Pita and Rita.

PETER: Excuse me, Rita, who's the guy in the green coat? Over by the food?

RITA: Oh... *(*RITA *sees the* OLD MAN.*)* Oh, yeah. I don't know.

MRS BOYLE: Everybody shmush together, come on! Marshall!... *(People crowd together around* PETER *and* RITA.*) Marshall!*

DR BOYLE: What?

MRS BOYLE: Get in the picture, come on!

DR BOYLE: Jesus Christ, I thought you were on fire.

MRS BOYLE: Get in, everybody! All right. Say "bullshit"! Smile!

("Bullshit". "Cheese". Flash.)

DR BOYLE: Don't tell her—

MRS BOYLE: Wait, I want to get another one. Don't move. Ohhhhh.

DR BOYLE: *(Overlapping, continuous from earlier line)* —you don't need a flashbulb in the middle of the day.

UNCLE FRED: My face hurts, hurry up!

MRS BOYLE: All right, say "Bullshit".

(*Again*)

AUNT DOROTHY: Oh, I had my face in a funny position.

UNCLE FRED: Whose fault is that?

AUNT DOROTHY: And don't say it's always that way.

PETER: Mom, who's the guy over by the bar?

MRS BOYLE: Who?

PETER: See who I mean?

MRS BOYLE: Oh...

(RITA *and the* OLD MAN *toast one another with their champagne.*)

RITA: Isn't he great?

MRS BOYLE: No, I thought he was with your firm.

PETER: (*Shaking his head*) Unh-uh.

(*The* OLD MAN *starts toward them.*)

MRS BOYLE: Marsh? Right behind me, don't look now, he's very peculiar.

DR BOYLE: Never seen him before in my life.

MRS BOYLE: He's not with the club, is he?

(*The* OLD MAN *comes up to them.*)

OLD MAN: Congratulations. Both of you.

RITA: Thank you.

PETER: Thank you very much.

TAYLOR: (*Extending his hand*) I'm Taylor McGowan.

OLD MAN: You make a lovely couple.

TAYLOR: Your name, I'm sorry?

OLD MAN: And what a wonderful day for it.

RITA: *(Mesmerized by him)* Yes.

(TAYLOR *shakes hands with the empty air.)*

TAYLOR: Good to meet you.

OLD MAN: How precious the time is... How little we realize 'til it's almost gone.

DR BOYLE: You'll have to forgive us, but none of us seems to remember who you are.

RITA: It's all right, Daddy.

OLD MAN: I only wanted to wish the two young people well. And perhaps to kiss the bride. Before I'm on my way.

DR BOYLE: Well—

RITA: I'd be flattered. Thank you.

TAYLOR: Some angle this guy's got.

RITA: My blessings to you.

(The OLD MAN *takes* RITA's *face in his hands. There is a low rumble which grows in volume as they begin to kiss. Wind rushes through the trees, leaves fall, no one moves except for* RITA, *whose bridal bouquet slips to the ground. The* OLD MAN *and* RITA *separate and the wind and rumble die down.)*

RITA: And you.

(The OLD MAN *seems off balance;* DR BOYLE *steadies him.)*

DR BOYLE: Do you want to sit down?

AUNT DOROTHY: Get him a chair, Fred.

TAYLOR: Too much blood rushing to the wrong place, I guess.

(The OLD MAN *stares at* PETER *and* RITA.*)*

DR BOYLE: Are you dizzy?

OLD MAN: Peter?...

(UNCLE FRED *brings a chair.*)

DR BOYLE: Here you go now.

(*He eases the* OLD MAN *into the chair, takes his pulse.*
PETER *remains fixated on the* OLD MAN. RITA *has
withdrawn from the crowd; she examines her dress, her
hands, the air around her, as if it were all new, miraculous.*)

MRS BOYLE: I thought you said you didn't know him.
(PETER *is mystified.*) Peter?

DR BOYLE: Take it easy now.

OLD MAN:
(*To* PETER)
Honey? Honey?... It's me.
What's happening?...   DR BOYLE:
Why is...? Why is   You're okay now, just
everybody...?   breathe for me, nice
                               and easy.

OLD MAN: (*Staring at* DR BOYLE) Daddy, it's me.

AUNT DOROTHY: Ohhhh, he thinks Marshall's his father.

TAYLOR: Where do you live, can you tell us?

DR BOYLE: Okay. He's doing fine. Everybody relax.

AUNT DOROTHY: Get him a glass of water, Fred.

DR BOYLE: He's had too much to drink, I suspect. Am I
right? A little too much champagne?

(*The* OLD MAN *begins to nod, strangely.*)

MRS BOYLE: Should I call an ambulance? Marshall?

DR BOYLE: No, no. He's going to be fine.

OLD MAN: I've had too much to drink.

DR BOYLE: That's right. Somebody get him a cup of
coffee.

(UNCLE FRED *arrives with water.*)

AUNT DOROTHY: Coffee, make it coffee.

MRS BOYLE: Where do you live, can you tell us?

OLD MAN: Please...

MRS BOYLE: Is there someone we can call?

OLD MAN: I'm sorry for any trouble I've caused.

(The OLD MAN *starts to stand.)*

DR BOYLE: There's no trouble.

MRS BOYLE: Don't let him, honey —

DR BOYLE: *(Overlapping)* We just want to see you don't hurt yourself.

UNCLE FRED: *(Returning with coffee)* Here you go.

OLD MAN: No, thank you.

(The OLD MAN *is backing away.)*

UNCLE FRED: Don't burn yourself.

OLD MAN: No.

AUNT DOROTHY: He doesn't want it, Fred.

MRS BOYLE: Don't just let him wander off is all I'm saying.

DR BOYLE: All right, Marion —

MRS BOYLE: He could fall and he could hurt himself, that's all —

DR BOYLE: He's not going to sue us, trust me.

(DR BOYLE and TAYLOR *follow the* OLD MAN *off.)*

MRS BOYLE: And find out where he lives!

UNCLE FRED: He'll be fine.

AUNT DOROTHY: I'm sure he's a neighbor or someone's gardener.

MRS BOYLE: Whose?

UNCLE FRED: *(Same time)* That's right.

MRS BOYLE: *(Starting to exit)* I know everyone in a five-mile radius.

AUNT DOROTHY: Marion, stay here.

UNCLE FRED: Marion —

AUNT DOROTHY: Go with her.

MRS BOYLE: He's not going to bite me, now stop it, Frederick, if you want to come, come.

(UNCLE FRED follows MRS BOYLE off.)

PETER: *(To RITA)* Are you all right? *(She nods.)* Are you sure?

AUNT DOROTHY: Oh, what a fuss. Forget all about it, pretend it never even happened.

PETER: We're okay, thanks.

AUNT DOROTHY: Don't you both look so wonderful, and you notice who he wanted to kiss, not me. Oh, you're going to have such a good time, where is it you're going again now? Marion told me.

(PETER waits for RITA to answer before:)

PETER: Jamaica.

AUNT DOROTHY: That's right. For how long?

PETER: Two weeks.

AUNT DOROTHY: Oh, they loved it there last year.... Your mom and dad... Well, I'm going to leave you two alone. Do you want another glass of champagne while I'm at the bar?

PETER: No, thanks.

AUNT DOROTHY: No?...

(AUNT DOROTHY moves off.)

PETER: That was so weird, wasn't it? Calling me honey? He just seemed so vulnerable. I swear I've never seen him before.... You're okay? *(RITA nods.)* You sure? You seem...kind of.... Okay.

(The others begin to filter back on.)

TAYLOR: *(Overlapping)* Unbelievable.

AUNT DOROTHY: What happened?

TAYLOR: Just took off down the street, kept going.

DR BOYLE: *(Overlapping)* Everything's fine now, it's all under control.

TAYLOR: *(To PETER)*
Guess he thought you were both kind of cute, huh?...

MRS BOYLE: Oh, my poor babies, to spoil your whole wedding.

AUNT DOROTHY: Have some champagne, Marion.

MRS BOYLE: No, my god, I'll throw up all those strawberries. *(To RITA)* Your father thinks that's the Evans' gardener, but I don't think it is, do you?...

DR BOYLE: *(Overlapping)* Enough, Marion.

MRS BOYLE: That's not the Evans' gardener, is it?... Rita?

(All eyes on RITA; she turns to look over her shoulder before turning back and smiling.)

RITA: Must have been my kiss is all.

AUNT DOROTHY: That's right.

| DR BOYLE: *(Overlapping)* | ~~UNCLE FRED:~~ |
| That's right. | There you go. |

RITA: Drives the men wild.

UNCLE FRED: Hear, hear!

| TAYLOR: | DR. BOYLE: *(To MRS BOYLE)* |
| This is a party, come on! | Come on, give me a kiss. |

MINISTER: A toast!

AUNT DOROTHY:	TAYLOR: *(Singing)*
Here's to the lucky	"Celebrate, celebrate!
couple!	Dance to the music!"

UNCLE FRED:	MINISTER:
Hear, hear!	To the lucky couple!

*(Someone starts to sing "For they're a jolly good couple!"
Everyone joins in, then singing fades.)*

PETER: *(To us, as he strips down to bathing trunks.)* And
there was a toast to us and to love and to Jamaica and to
our plane flight and to airline safety and to the old
drunk whoever he was. Whoever he was. I was
completely trashed by the time the limo pulled up to
take us to the airport. Dr. Boyle told us to sign anything
we wanted onto the hotel bill, his treat, and off we
went.... The whole way down on the plane and straight
through that first night in the hotel, Rita slept like a
baby. I couldn't. For some reason. I kept hearing that
poor old guy calling me "Honey". "Honey, it's me."
Who's "me"? And I'd wanted to protect him. *(Pause)* In
the morning we headed down to the pool, husband and
wife.

(Jamaica. Poolside. The WAITER *stands beside* PETER *and*
RITA, *both in chaise lounges.* PETER *holds a drink in a
coconut shell, decorated with a paper umbrella.)*

PETER: *(To* RITA*)* Don't you want to try one?

RITA: *(To the* WAITER*)* Just a seltzer water.

PETER: Okay. *(To the* WAITER*)* I'll take another, thanks.
(The WAITER *retreats. Beat.* PETER *notices something on*
RITA*'s wrist.)* What's that?

RITA: You like?

PETER: Well...sure, where'd you get it?

RITA: Just now.

PETER: In the shop? Here? It's not gold, is it?

RITA: Fourteen carat.

PETER: You're kidding. How much was it?

RITA: Fifteen hundred or so.

PETER: Dollars?

RITA: Why? He said to charge anything.

PETER: You charged fifteen hundred dollars on your dad's bill?

RITA: I like it.

PETER: Well... You do? It's sort of like a...it's like a charm bracelet, isn't it?

RITA: It is a charm bracelet.

PETER: Like old women wear? I'm sorry. Look, if you like it, I think it's great. And he did say.... You're right, he's your dad.

RITA: Relax, we're on vacation.

PETER: I know.

RITA: And you're my puppy puppy.

PETER: Your puppy puppy?

RITA: And the world is a wonderful place to live, admit it!... Do my back?

(He takes the sunscreen, looks at it before applying it.)

PETER: Twenty-five?... I keep thinking about that crazy old schmuck from the wedding.

RITA: Mmmm, that feels good, darling!

PETER: Who do you suppose he was?

RITA: Hm?

PETER: The old guy.

RITA: Oh, I don't know.... My fairy godfather come to sprinkle the fairy dust on us.

PETER: Aren't you curious?

RITA: Nope. Come for a swim.

PETER: You just put the stuff on.

RITA: I know. Come on, I'll race you!

(She runs off.)

PETER: *(To us)* Our first full day being married and she seemed like a different Rita. I told myself, It's the excitement. And, come on, it's the rest of your life, you want it to be wonderful. It's natural to ask, "Is this the right person for me? Am I the right person for her?... Who the hell is she, anyway?"

(RITA returns, dripping wet.)

RITA: Oh, I love it here, don't you? *(Singing as she dries herself)* "Yellow bird, so high in banana tree..."

PETER: Are you sorry you married me?... Rita, you were supposed to laugh.

RITA: Oh, shut up.

PETER: Okay.

RITA: I want to go jet-skiing and I want to go scuba-diving and I want to go up into the mountains and see the monkeys, okay? And maybe go to a soccer game? *(She plants a noisy kiss on him.)* With you on my arm.

(Beat)

PETER: Do you ever think how we're each a whole, separate being beside one another. Each with a heart pumping inside and a soul and all our memories.

How I can never, no matter how close we ever become, share your past, be with you as a nine-year-old, as a baby.

RITA: Don't worry about it, all right?

PETER: I wasn't.

RITA: Just take things as they come and enjoy them. That's what life's for.

PETER: You're right. You're absolutely right.

(Pause. RITA catches PETER staring at her.)

RITA: Feast away!

PETER: All right, I wasn't going to bring this up, but.... Now just hear me out first; I know what you're going to say, but.... Okay. You know how you never get any time to work on your portfolio and— Well, now that we have just the one rent, what if—just for a while, not forever—you quit tending bar and let me support you.

RITA: Sure.

PETER: What? You'd consider it?

RITA: Why not?

PETER: Really?

RITA: Let you bring home the bacon for a while. Right?

PETER: Right.

RITA: If it'd make you happy.

PETER: Baby, I'm sorry, I'm freaking out. Are you sorry you married me?

RITA: No. *(Remembering)* Oh. Ha-ha-ha.

PETER: I'm serious this time.

RITA: Don't be a silly.

PETER: Okay. Okay. *(To us) Not* okay. The days went by.
We went to the soccer game, we windsurfed, or
windfell, we ate, we snorkeled, we walked on the
beach, always under a ton of sunscreen. And Rita was
tireless. Fearless. And sleeping, not that there was
anything wrong with that. No, no. Nothing was
wrong—exactly. But nothing felt...nothing *felt. (Pause)*
About a week into the vacation...

(The pool. The WAITER *stands beside them.)*

WAITER: Something from the bar?

RITA: Another seltzer, please, and clean this up, would
you, it's drawing flies.

PETER: Oh, I'll have a Long Island Ice Tea this time,
thanks. *(The* WAITER *moves off.)* Doesn't it ever bother
you sometimes, though? The black/white thing? I
mean, it's so obviously a class issue here, not that it isn't
in New York. But you'd think they'd all just rise up and
kill us all poolside.

RITA: Why is that?

PETER: Because. We have the money and they don't.

RITA: We worked for it, didn't we?

PETER: Well, your father worked for it, in this case.
But, I mean, you talk about the world being so
precarious, everything ending in a blinding flash; it
would seem a little less likely if things were a little
more egalitarian, wouldn't it? If there were a slightly
more equal distribution of the wealth, that's all.

RITA: You want to give 'em your money, go ahead.

PETER: No, I... Why would you—?

RITA: Peter, you're doing it again.

PETER: I know.

RITA: You take a perfect situation and you pee all over it. Be happy.

PETER: Okay, I was just referring to the people we saw living in abandoned cars and refrigerators out by the airport.

RITA: That was terrible. But you don't have to look at it, do you?

PETER: Oh, good attitude... Look, I'm just trying to make conversation, Rita, you're the Commie in the woodpile, not me.

(Beat)

RITA: Whatcha reading?

PETER: The case histories? Freud.

RITA: Oh. Sounds interesting. Can I read it when you're through?

(PETER stares at her. The WAITER returns.)

WAITER: I'm sorry, Sir, the bartender say he don't know what that is.

PETER: A Long Island Ice Tea? *(To RITA)* What goes into one?... Rita? An Ice Tea? How do you make it?

RITA: I'm sorry, darling, I've forgotten.

PETER: What, do you have it all written down behind the bar or something?

RITA: I'm on vacation.

PETER: So you can't remember a drink recipe for something I'd like to order?

RITA: *(Overlapping)* Yes. That's right. On the money. Bingo! It's a real busman's holiday with you around, you know? You could fuck up a wet dream!

(She walks off. Beat.)

PETER: *(To the* WAITER*)* Nothing right now, thanks.
(To us) It's one thing to forget a drink recipe or a book
you read a long time ago, maybe, *maybe,* but your *ideals*?
It was as if she had switched channels, switched...
something. (Pause) Our last night we walked out on the
beach in a light mist...like cloth being pulled across
your skin.

(The beach. They walk.)

RITA: Oh, it's so beautiful, isn't it? It's great to be alive.
And young. There will never be a more perfect night.
Or a better chance for two people to love each other.
If they don't try so hard. *(Beat)* I remembered the recipe
for Long Island Ice Tea. White rum, vodka—

PETER: You don't have to prove anything to me, Rita.
(Pause) You know...I was thinking about you growing
up. What— Like, what was it like having a surgeon for
a father?

RITA: Oh...well, it was nice. I always thought, "He helps
people."

PETER: What about your brothers and sisters? How did
they feel about it?

RITA: You'd have to ask them.

PETER: *(To us)* Nobody's memory is that bad! Or was
she toying with me? That wasn't like her at all. Unless
something was terribly, terribly wrong.

RITA: Peter? Make love to me.

PETER: Here?

RITA: No one'll see. I want to have your baby.... I want
your baby inside me.

PETER: You don't know how that makes me feel.

RITA: Yes I do.

PETER: You don't want babies, don't you remember? You've read Freud's case histories and your father's a dentist, not a surgeon. You don't have brothers and sisters.

RITA: Why are you telling me all this?...

PETER: What, you were teasing me?

RITA: Of course I was teasing you. Did you think I didn't know those things?... Sweetie?

PETER: You never call me that or "Puppy puppy", you never say "Don't be a silly" or "Bring home the bacon" or pull the skin off your chicken. You're not drinking, you're not using salt, Rita, you're suddenly—

RITA: I want to have your baby. I'm taking better care of myself. Now, please, darling, relax. You're having some kind of a—

PETER: No. No! You're a Communist, Rita, or Socialist, Democrat, whatever you are, you don't defend the social order in Jamaica or anywhere, you have.... You're just not.... You're not...*you*. It's like you don't even need me anymore.

RITA: You need to take a hot bath and look at the moon and breathe life in.

PETER: Rita is afraid of life, she doesn't drink it in.

RITA: I'm going to insist that you see someone as soon as we get back to New York.

PETER: Je hebt erg witte tanden.

RITA: Thanks.

PETER: What did I say?

RITA: You said my teeth are white, you know what you said.

PETER: *(Embracing her)* Yes! Thank you. My baby. What do you say?

RITA: What do you mean?

PETER: What's your line? What do you say? Your line, you memorized it.

RITA: I'm sorry, Peter —

PETER: *(Overlapping)* In Dutch! Rita, what do you say?

RITA: I say goodnight.

(She turns, starts to walk off; he grabs her.)

PETER: No, please! Rita!

RITA: *(Overlapping)* Hey! Watch it, pal!

PETER: I want you to be you, Rita, I want you!

RITA: I am me. This is all I am. I'm sorry I can't be whatever you want me to be. This is me. And maybe what you saw wasn't here at all.

(She walks off. Pause. PETER looks at us. The sound of surf breaking. Lights fade.)

ACT TWO

(The BOYLE *home.)*

MRS BOYLE: Peter!

DR BOYLE: There they are.

MRS BOYLE: Don't you both look wonderful.

DR BOYLE: Not much of a tan here.

PETER: Well, we decided not to age on this trip.

MRS BOYLE: Well, you both look wonderful.

DR BOYLE: Rested.

PETER: That's right.

MRS BOYLE: *(To* RITA*)* Did you sleep? *(*RITA *nods.)* Ohhhh.

PETER: Like a baby. Every night straight through.

DR BOYLE: Well, you're having a good effect on her.

RITA: It's so good to see you both.

MRS BOYLE: What'll you drink? Beer?

RITA: Nothing for me, thank you, Mom.

DR BOYLE: Peter?

PETER: Sure, thanks. Rita's quit drinking.

MRS BOYLE: Ohhh. Really?

DR BOYLE: Wonderful.

MRS BOYLE: So now tell us everything.

RITA: It was terrific.

PETER: It was just great and we can't thank you enough.

MRS BOYLE: How was the weather?

RITA: Perfect.

PETER: Oh, yeah. Really.

DR BOYLE: Did you get any golf in there?

RITA: That was the one thing we didn't quite get to, I'm afraid.

MRS BOYLE: *(To* PETER*)* He's teasing her.

DR BOYLE: We took Rita for golf lessons every year for I don't know how many years —

MRS BOYLE: Three.

DR BOYLE: Or four.

MRS BOYLE: Three.

DR BOYLE: Three. Okay.

RITA: Well —

DR BOYLE: *(Overlapping)* She never got with it.

RITA: Maybe I'll try it again. I'm serious, I might like to.

(Beat)

MRS BOYLE: Did you go snorkeling?

RITA: Oh, sure.

PETER: You name it, we tried it. Rita even wanted to go up on one of those kites — that they haul from behind the boats?

MRS BOYLE: Oh, you're kidding. No!

RITA: Peter was upset by all the poverty, wanted to give them all our money.

(DR *and* MRS BOYLE *turn and stare at* PETER.)

PETER: Oh, show them the bracelet you bought, Rita.

(RITA *shakes her head.*)

RITA: I didn't bring it.

PETER: Ohhh, too bad.

MRS BOYLE: I want to see.

PETER: It's gold. It's incredible. All these big things hanging down from it, must weigh about a ton....

MRS BOYLE: Sounds expen—

DR BOYLE: *(Overlapping)* But you know, that's the reality— Excuse me— You can't escape it, wherever you go. *(Pause)* Poverty.

MRS BOYLE: No.

RITA: That's what I told him.

DR BOYLE: It's reality.

(Pause)

MRS BOYLE: Oh, speaking of which, that man from the wedding, Rita— Your father told me not to bring it up, but—was not the Evans' gardener. I called up over there after you left for the airport.

DR BOYLE: All right, enough.

PETER: Who do you think he was, though?

RITA: I told you, I thought he was my fairy godfather.

DR BOYLE: That's right.

(Pause)

PETER: Strange.

MRS BOYLE: *(To* RITA*)* Well... Why don't we let the men talk about whatever it is men talk about and you can help me set the table?

RITA: Great. Fun.

MRS BOYLE: And I can show you the sketch I did of your father in class. We'll be ready to eat in about fifteen minutes, gents.

PETER: Terrific.

(RITA *follows* MRS BOYLE *off.*)

DR BOYLE: When do you start work?

PETER: Tomorrow.

DR BOYLE: You folks gonna have enough room in that apartment of Rita's?

PETER: Oh sure.

DR BOYLE: Another beer there?

(PETER *shakes his head. Beat.*)

PETER: Does Rita...? She seem okay to you?

DR BOYLE: Why, something the matter?

PETER: No. No.

DR BOYLE: Tell me, for godsake.

PETER: No. She seems changed a little bit.

DR BOYLE: Well, you're married now. And you're dealing with a slippery entity there.

PETER: Uh-huh.

DR BOYLE: She's always had the highest expectations of everybody. Especially herself. But... I don't know, in some way she's always been...uncertain. Drove her mother and me crazy for a while.

PETER: Yeah, she told me a little bit. Her politics and stuff.

DR BOYLE: Politics?

PETER: Oh...n —

DR BOYLE: *(Overlapping)* What politics?

PETER: No, no, I was mixing it up with something else....

DR BOYLE: You'll get used to her. She's young. You're both young.

PETER: She gets, you know, really forgetful sometimes.

DR BOYLE: I know.

PETER: Forgets whole...

DR BOYLE: Years. I'm aware.

PETER: She's given up salt, too.

DR BOYLE: Oh, she has. I've got to do that.

PETER: And she pulls the skin off her chicken.

DR BOYLE: Oh. Well, she's way ahead of me. Watching out for her old age already...

(Pause)

PETER: She's thinking of maybe quitting her job at the bar, too, so....

DR BOYLE: She is.

PETER: Yeah. So I can support us.

DR BOYLE: Outstanding. You must be making her very happy. Congratulations...

PETER: Thanks.

(PETER's office)

TAYLOR: Hey!

PETER: Hey!

TAYLOR: No tan.

PETER: No tan.

TAYLOR: We missed you.

PETER: Thanks.

TAYLOR: Welcome back. Listen, Kollegger wants to know what happened to April.

PETER: Oh. The N.I.H. never sent the documents.

TAYLOR: Oh. What do I tell him?

PETER: Tell him the N.I.H. never sent the documents.

TAYLOR: *(Overlapping)* — never sent the documents. I like the angle.

(TAYLOR *starts to leave.*)

PETER: Listen, Tay?

TAYLOR: Yeah.

PETER: If you could switch souls with somebody?... Like go inside their body and they go inside yours?... You know? Switch?

TAYLOR: ...Yeeaaaaah?

PETER: Do you think it would be possible, if you didn't know someone, to impersonate them, by just being inside them and...looking like them?

TAYLOR: Where are they?

PETER: Inside you.

TAYLOR: And you're inside them?

PETER: Right.

TAYLOR: Why would you go inside another person's body if you didn't know them?

PETER: It's conjecture.

TAYLOR: I think I know that, Peter. But wouldn't you do better to pick someone you knew, a particular person you envied —

PETER: Right.

TAYLOR: —or admired so that you could do or be or have the things this other person did or bee'd or had?

PETER: Maybe. Yes.

TAYLOR: Are you Rita now? Is that what you're telling me? You two have merged?

PETER: All right, here's another question. Have you ever... This is sort of a bizarre question. Have you ever been having sex with somebody...?

TAYLOR: Nope.

PETER: And they're doing everything, you know, right more or less.

TAYLOR: Oh, right, sex, I remember, go ahead.

PETER: And you just get the feeling that...something is wrong? I mean, they pretty much stop doing some of the things they used to do—

TAYLOR: Ohhhh.

PETER: —and only do certain other things now, more...

TAYLOR: Right.

PETER: ...traditional sorts of things.

TAYLOR: Blow jobs, you mean.

PETER: No, I'm not talking about anything specific.

TAYLOR: No one likes to do that.

PETER: Well, that happens not to be strictly the case, but....

TAYLOR: No woman has ever enjoyed doing that, I'm just telling you. It's common knowledge.

PETER: You haven't had sex, but you know all about it.

TAYLOR: Hey, you asked me.

PETER: Yes, I know I did.

TAYLOR: I'm just trying to help.

PETER: Thank you. A lot.

TAYLOR: Welcome back.

PETER: Great talking to ya. *(To us)* That night everything was miraculously restored....

*(*RITA *and* PETER's *apartment.)*

RITA: Hi.

PETER: Hi.

RITA: How was work?

PETER: Okay.

RITA: It was?... Making you a surprise.

PETER: What?

RITA: Guess.

PETER: I can't. What's this?

RITA:Dewar's.

PETER: What, you're back on the sauce? What's the surprise? *(She sniffs the air; he does too.)* Spaetzles? *(*RITA *smiles.)* You're kidding.

RITA: I'm sure they won't be anywhere near as good as Sophie's, but then I'm not such a cruel mama, either. You want a Molson?

PETER: Sure.

(She goes off; he picks up a book.)

RITA: *(From off)* So, I don't know, I made some calls about taking my portfolio around today, but the whole thing terrifies me.... *(She returns with his Molson.)* And I started reading that, finally.

PETER: *The White Hotel?*

RITA: Cheers.

PETER: Cheers.

RITA: You didn't call the doctor, did you?

PETER: No, I will.

RITA: No, I don't want you to.... I know things were hard in Jamaica. Maybe it's taken me this time to get used to being married, but...I love you, Peter.

(They kiss. He pulls away, holding on to her.)

PETER: You read her journal, didn't you? You figured out how to fix your hair from the pictures in the albums and what to wear, what she drinks.... Where is she? Please. I won't be angry. You can go back wherever you came from and I won't tell a soul, you don't have to tell me who you are. Just tell me where Rita is and we'll pretend this never took place. *(Pause)* Okay. Play it your way. But I'm on to you.

(PETER walks out.)

(The Tin Market. The OLD MAN is seated as PETER enters.)

TOM: Hey, Pete, you're back. How was your honeymoon?

PETER: Good, thanks.

TOM: How's Reet?

PETER: Great.

TOM: Where is she?

PETER: Oh, not feeling too well, actually. Let me have a double vodka on the rocks....

TOM: Got your postcard.

PETER: Yeah?

(PETER sees the OLD MAN.)

TOM: There you go. It's on the house. *(PETER does not respond.)* Don't mention it. *(To the* OLD MAN*)* Dewars?

(The OLD MAN *nods.)*

PETER: Is he a regular?

TOM: Oh, yeah, last couple of weeks or so, I guess. Why? You know him?

(PETER downs his drink as TOM *takes the* OLD MAN *his.* PETER *crosses to the* OLD MAN*'s table.)*

PETER: Have we... Have we met? *(The* OLD MAN *nods.)* Mind if I sit? *(He does.)* You were at my wedding, weren't you? *(The* OLD MAN *nods. Beat.)* Do I know you? *(The* OLD MAN *nods.)* What's my stepmother's name?...

OLD MAN: *(Unable to remember)* Uhhh...

PETER: What's the movie I said I was going to see the night I left for Europe?...

OLD MAN: *The Wild Bunch!*

PETER: Je hebt erg witte tanden.

OLD MAN: Not anymore.

(He shows PETER *his teeth.)*

PETER: What shape's your father's shrapnel scar?

OLD MAN: He thinks it's shaped like a saxophone, but it's not.

PETER: I knew it wasn't you! I *knew* it. Oh, I knew it! Oh my god, Rita.

(They embrace.)

OLD MAN: Baby.

PETER: Oh... *(Beat.* PETER *pulls back.)* ...god... Maybe we shouldn't.... Maybe... How much do we owe you here, Tom?

TOM: No, man, it's on the house.

PETER: Oh, okay, great. Great. *(To the* OLD MAN*)* Okay? *(To* TOM*)* I'm just gonna walk the old guy down to the subway.

TOM: Okay.

PETER: Good to see you, Tom.

TOM: You, too. Tell Rita I hope she feels better.

PETER: I will. I will. *(To the* OLD MAN*)* Come on, let's get out of here.

(Outside. They walk.)

PETER: How are you?

OLD MAN: I've missed you.

PETER: Where have you been?

OLD MAN: Brooklyn. In Borough Park. I stayed with his family. Julius Becker. He had his wallet on him. I didn't know what else to do, where to go; I couldn't call my mother or go to the police. Who would believe me, right?

PETER: Let's head back toward the apartment. Okay?

OLD MAN: They could throw me into an institution or an old folks' home; I didn't even have our keys. I had to pretend to be him until you figured it out. And I knew you would.

PETER: I think this is like one of those dreams where you tell yourself, Just hang on, and we're all gonna wake up. We'll walk in and she'll be there and it's gonna be okay, Rita.

OLD MAN: I just keep thinking there's something I'm forgetting.... When he leaned in to kiss me I saw this

look in his eye, you know? And something.... I've got to
slow down, I'm sorry.

PETER: That's okay.

(They slow their pace.)

OLD MAN: I get short of breath.

PETER: Better?

OLD MAN: What was I saying?

PETER: You get short of breath.

OLD MAN: Before that. Peter, I'm not senile.

PETER: I know, I know.

OLD MAN: I was holding your hand and then I wasn't.
I was turned all around. You were over there and I was
over there. I thought it was a mirror, that's why I
reached out — to steady myself, and instead I saw his
hand...this hand...on me.... And then everybody was
staring at me and my dad was saying I'd had too much
to drink and I don't know, I thought I had salmonella.

PETER: Really? That's great.

OLD MAN: I thought if I went along with it, then you'd
all come running out after me and say, "It's a joke, come
on, Rita, you're going on your honeymoon." And we'd
laugh.... I just kept walking, past all the cars parked for
the wedding. I was afraid to look down at my shadow
to see if it was true — my reflection in the windows.... I
found this card in his wallet. *(He shows* PETER *the card.)*
"In case of emergency, please notify Mr. and Mrs.
Jerome Blier." His daughter and her husband. They
came and picked me up.... *(Beat)* So how was our
honeymoon? *(*PETER *does not laugh.)* Oh, come on!

PETER: I'm fine.

OLD MAN: Does he know you know?

PETER: HE? Yeah. He does.

OLD MAN: She. Whatever. He does?

PETER: Yes, I think so.

(They have stopped walking. They look up at the apartment.)

OLD MAN: Is he there now?

PETER: *(Nodding)* I think maybe you should wait outside in the hall in case he tries to bolt. All right?

OLD MAN: Peter?

PETER: What?... I know, come on.

(The apartment. PETER enters. The OLD MAN stands outside the open door.)

PETER: Rita?

(DR BOYLE emerges from the bedroom with a suitcase; the OLD MAN recedes out of sight.)

DR BOYLE: Peter.

PETER: What's the matter? Where's Rita?

DR BOYLE: I'm sorry about all this, Peter.

PETER: Did something happen?

DR BOYLE: You know I am. You know I like you.

PETER: What do you mean you're sorry?

DR BOYLE: Rita's gone back to New Jersey with her mother, Peter.

PETER: Why?

DR BOYLE: I think it would be best if you didn't come out to the house or call for a while until she calms down.

PETER: I went for a walk. Calms down?

DR BOYLE: We brought both cars so I could pick up some of her things. And I'll be out of your way momentarily.

PETER: Wait a minute, Dr. Boyle, I'm....

DR BOYLE: I'm sorry for whatever personal turmoil you're going through, Peter.

PETER: Turmoil? What did she tell you?

DR BOYLE: If you want me to refer you to somebody.... Rita says you're suffering from delusions, Peter. And I should tell you she's talking about filing for a divorce or an annulment, whichever would be —

PETER: What? Wait.

DR BOYLE: *(Overlapping, continuous)* — most appropriate under the circumstances. I'm awfully sorry.

PETER: What circumstances? What sort of delusions did she say I was suffering from?

DR BOYLE: Rita...

PETER: Go on. I want to hear this.

DR BOYLE: She was hysterical, Peter, when she called us.

PETER: What did she say?

DR BOYLE: Rita says you're convinced that she's someone else.

PETER: Someone — ? What, and you believe that? What does that mean? Dr. Boyle, I went for a walk. We had a — Okay, we had a fight. I went out. You and Mrs. Boyle never have fights? We had a difference of opinion.

DR BOYLE: I practically had to carry her to the car. Are you telling me that nothing else has happened between the two of you? Nothing at all?

PETER: Seriously, Marshall, think about what you're saying. Rita... You're —

DR BOYLE: *(Overlapping)* If you'd seen that girl's face — I'm sorry, I'm just — I'm going to have to defer to my daughter's wishes.

PETER: I can't believe this. You're just going to take her word?

DR BOYLE: It's a little difficult to believe...knowing Rita as I do, Son, that this —

PETER: You don't know her.

DR BOYLE: *(Overlapping, continuous)* — is all about a squabble, a tiff as you say.

PETER: *(Overlapping)* You don't know anything about her, that's the absurd part. You don't know your own flesh and blood.

DR BOYLE: Well, I'm sure you're right.

(DR BOYLE starts to leave; PETER halts him.)

PETER: Rita was a Communist, did you know that? That she was in a Communist — Socialist party? And, all right, here's something else you don't know: We didn't go out for a year. We didn't go out for anything like a year; we went out for two months — at that point, six weeks. We haven't known each other six months now! You wouldn't know if she was lying to you, because you don't know her; you only see what you want to see. And she's lying to you now, Dr. Boyle, she may know certain facts —

DR BOYLE: Let go of my sleeve, please.

PETER: *(Under, continuous)* — but that's from reading Rita's journals! She doesn't — Watch her! Watch the way she sits! Her eyes!

DR BOYLE: See a doctor, Boy, all —

PETER: *(Overlapping)* Rita— Watch the way she listens to everything we say, the way she *chews* for godsake, it isn't her! Open your eyes!

DR BOYLE: I'd like to leave now, Peter. *(Beat)* Thank you.

(He goes out.)

PETER: This isn't happening.

(The OLD MAN *returns.)*

OLD MAN: He didn't see me.

PETER: Look...I like you very much. I'm not equipped for this. I'm sorry. I still like you.

OLD MAN: *Like* me?

PETER: I'm not...I don't feel the same way about you, I'm sorry. I'm not attracted to you.

OLD MAN: What, are you nuts? I don't think that's the issue, Peter, have a seat, come on, you're—

PETER: If I thought that you were really here, Rita... What's the name of the guy you went out with in high school? Wait. You told me once—Rita did—but I've forgotten. And if I can't remember, then you can't. The one who wanted to run away.

OLD MAN: John.

PETER: Oh Rita. *(Beat)* It could have been in my unconscious. You know that. You've read Freud. Haven't you?

OLD MAN: You're not imagining me. Or we're both insane....

PETER: All right, *think.* We've got to try to figure out how.... This just does not happen.

OLD MAN: Tell me about it.

PETER: All right...let me see his wallet, please. May I?
(The OLD MAN *hands over the wallet.)* Thank you.
Becker? Is he Dutch, do you know?

OLD MAN: Is it a Dutch name?

PETER: You're the one who says you live there, Rita,
Jesus!

OLD MAN: Well, they don't speak Dutch. I mean, I can't
exactly ask. I'm trying to keep a low profile in case they
find out I'm really a girl, okay?

*(*PETER *has rifled through the wallet's contents, found the
card.)*

PETER: How do you say the daughter's name?

OLD MAN: Blier. Leah and Jerry. Why?

*(*PETER *picks up the phone, starts to dial.)*

PETER: How old?

OLD MAN: Old, I don't know, you know. Forty?... What
are you doing?

(Phone rings. LEAH *enters, carrying receiver.)*

LEAH: Hello?

PETER: Hello, Mrs. Jerome Blier?

LEAH: Yes?

PETER: Hi, my name is Larry...White from the Delancey
Street Human Resource and Crisis Intervention Center.
Is your father a Mr. Julius Becker?

LEAH: Is something wrong?

PETER: No, no, he's right here, Mrs. Blier.

LEAH: He is?

PETER: Yes, he's fine, he's in good hands.

LEAH: *(Overlapping)* What happened, please? Where — ?

PETER: *(Overlapping)* Nothing's happened, Mrs. Blier.
He apparently walked up to a couple of young
gentlemen and, uh, asked them if they knew what city
he was in and they were kind enough to call us here at
the hotline.

LEAH: I see.

PETER: But your father's here now and he seems to be
fine.

LEAH: Where are you, let me write it down. My
husband's—

PETER: *(Overlapping)* I'd like to ask you a few questions
first if that's all right.

LEAH: My husband's gone to move the car. I'm sorry.

PETER: Where was your father born, Mrs. Blier?

LEAH: Oh, in Amsterdam. Nobody seems to know the
exact year.

PETER: And is he on any medications?

LEAH: He's done this before, you know.

PETER: He has.

LEAH: Two weeks ago he disappeared. We had to go
and pick him up in New Jersey.

PETER: Was there some reason? Did he know someone
there?

LEAH: Not that I'm aware of, no.

PETER: Are you sure?

LEAH: No.

PETER: Is your father suffering from any mental or
neurologic disorders, Mrs. Blier?

LEAH: He's been.... He hasn't been himself since my
mother died last fall.

PETER: I see.

LEAH: Then he had to move in with us.... I'm sorry, is he there now?

PETER: Yes.

LEAH: Could I speak to him, please?

PETER: Well, I'd like to finish filling out my form —

LEAH: *(Overlapping)* I won't be a moment.... Please.

PETER: All right. Hang on. *(To the* OLD MAN*)* Mr. Becker, it's your daughter.

(The OLD MAN *shakes his head vigorously.)*

OLD MAN: *(Loud, for* LEAH*'s benefit:)* Who?

PETER: She'd like to talk to you. Your daughter!

(The OLD MAN *takes the receiver.)*

LEAH: Daddy?... Daddy?

OLD MAN: Yes?

LEAH: It's Leah. Are you all right?

OLD MAN: I'm fine.

LEAH: Where are you?

OLD MAN: I'm here.

LEAH: Where did you go?

OLD MAN: I didn't go anywhere.

LEAH: Now you stay there.

OLD MAN: I'm not going anywhere.

LEAH: And you do what the man says.

OLD MAN: Oh, stop worrying about it.

LEAH: All right. I love you.

OLD MAN: Don't worry about it.

LEAH: All right, let me talk to the...

OLD MAN: *(Under, to* PETER*)* Here, you talk to her.

(The OLD MAN *hands* PETER *the phone.)*

PETER: *(Into the receiver)* Mrs. Blier?

LEAH: Yes?

PETER: Is there anything about your father's condition, is there any reason why he might —

LEAH: I can't put him in a home!...

PETER: No one's suggesting that you put your father in a home, Mrs. Blier, not at all.

LEAH: I'm sorry. I didn't mean to burden you with any of this.

PETER: You're not burdening anyone.

LEAH: We found out he has lung cancer three months ago. And cirrhosis he's had for years. I can't put him away. He doesn't even have a year to live. You know?... If you knew the man he used to be. He ran his own stationery store for forty-seven years. *(Beat)* Let me have your address, please.

PETER: I'm going to have to call you back, Mrs. Blier.

LEAH: Well, wait, my husband's just gone to park the car.

PETER: *(Overlapping)* No, I'm sorry, I'm — I will, I'll call you back.

(He hangs up.)

LEAH: Hello?

*(*LEAH *disappears.)*

OLD MAN: What? What's the matter?... What did she say?

PETER: Nothing.

OLD MAN: Am I sick?

PETER: No.

OLD MAN: This is me, Peter, remember?

(Pause)

PETER: You have lung cancer. And cirrhosis. She said she thought you had a year to live.

(Pause)

OLD MAN: Well... Am I Dutch, anyway?... Okay, first thing, we need a plan. What does he think happened to me? Where does he think I am? Maybe he doesn't think. Maybe it wasn't intentional. Is that possible?

PETER: It was intentional.

OLD MAN: Maybe it's some form of hypnosis. *(Pause)* All right, here's what we know: He wouldn't have called my parents if he was going to disappear. Obviously he wants to be me. Why?... Well, who wouldn't? He doesn't know I've found you, so I probably shouldn't go outside in case he's spying on us and Leah will definitely go to the police anyway, so.... My dad isn't going to leave me alone with you for a while, I know that. Mom's the one who's going to want us back together; she's crazy about you, and she isn't going to want me around the house, and she certainly won't believe what I'm telling her, she never does, so.... I say that our best bet is try and get her to bring him here. Don't you?

PETER: He'll scream.

OLD MAN: Let him. The last time somebody broke into one of these apartments, they used a blowtorch and nobody even called — I mean, I had a fire in the kitchen once and went screaming out into the hall. Nobody even opened their doors.... We'll think of something. *(Pause)* Okay?...

(Pause)

PETER: *(To us)* The next six days were the worst, the strangest of my life. I called in sick. We moved back and forth from room to room. We played cards, I cooked, we watched TV. It was as if we'd been married forever, suddenly, without the sex. At night I could feel the loneliness coming off of both of us like heat. The third day I called her parents; no answer. I tried again later — the same. The next day, same. After dark we went out to the house; not a sign. We used the spare key to get in; a few suitcases missing, according to Rita, that was all. The next night, still nothing. I called Rita's Aunt Dorothy in Cincinnati. She had no idea where they were and wanted to know why I didn't know. I told her Rita and I had split up. She was sorry to hear it. Rita and I, meanwhile, kept up the pleasantries, the old married couple we'd become.

(The apartment. PETER stares at the TV.)

OLD MAN: Something to eat?... Maybe I should teach myself to cook now that I've got the time. What do you think?

PETER: Great.

OLD MAN: Who's winning? *(PETER shrugs.)* Who's playing? *(PETER shrugs again.)* Well...

PETER: Rita?

OLD MAN: What?

PETER: What if they never come back?... What if they're gone forever?

OLD MAN: Well...

PETER: I miss your face.

OLD MAN: Don't think about it.

PETER: How soft it was.

(Pause)

OLD MAN: I miss it, too.

PETER: Your hair was so great.

OLD MAN: Oh, come on.

PETER: And your little white feet.

OLD MAN: What, you don't like these? *(Pause)* You know...if you think how we're born and we go through all the struggle of growing up and learning the multiplication tables and the name for everything, the rules, how not to get run over, braid your hair, pig-Latin. Figuring out how to sneak out of the house late at night. Just all the ins and outs, the *effort*, and learning to accept all the flaws in everybody and everything. And then getting a job, probably something you don't even like doing for not enough money, like bartending, and that's if you're lucky. That's if you're not born in Calcutta or Ecuador or the U.S. without money. Then there's your marriage and raising your own kids if...you know. And they're going through the same struggle all over again, only worse, because somebody's trying to sell them crack in the first grade by now. And all this time you're paying taxes and your hair starts to fall out and you're wearing six pairs of glasses which you can never find and you can't recognize yourself in the mirror and your parents die and your friends, again, if you're lucky, and it's not you first. And if you live long enough, you finally get to watch everybody die: all your loved ones, your wife, your husband and your kids, maybe, and you're totally alone. And as a final reward for all this...you disappear. *(Pause)* No one knows where. *(Pause)* So we might as well have a good time while we're here, don't you think?

PETER: I don't want you to die, Rita.

OLD MAN: I don't want me to die, either. And I'm going to. So are you. Hopefully later and not sooner. But we got to have this. I mean, what a trip! Meeting you and being in love. Falling. It was bitchin' for a while. And okay, so this isn't such a turn on, I admit. But...

PETER: I adore you.

OLD MAN: What? My hearing. No, I'm serious.

PETER: I said *I adore you!*

OLD MAN: That's what I thought.

PETER: For better or for worse.

OLD MAN: Huh?

PETER: I said: You would have hated Jamaica. Trust me.

(The OLD MAN *rises, crosses to* PETER. PETER *stands. They face one another for a moment.* PETER *can't bring himself to kiss the* OLD MAN. *The* OLD MAN *hands* PETER *the phone.)*

OLD MAN: Try again.

*(*PETER *dials. Phone rings.* MRS BOYLE *enters with receiver.)*

MRS BOYLE: Hello?

PETER: Oh, Marion, it's Peter.

MRS BOYLE: I thought it might be you.

PETER: Where've you been? I've been worried. How's Rita?

MRS BOYLE: They've just run down to the store; I may have to get off. She's terrible, Peter. We took her to London. She was so shook up, Marshall thought she needed a rest. I don't know, I was tempted to call you from over there, but I didn't, I'm sorry.

PETER: Is she okay?

MRS BOYLE: What happened between the two of you, Peter? If you don't want to tell me you don't have to.

PETER: No, I do, I just am not sure I know. I said—I guess I must have said something about her not being the same person. And then I lost my temper with Dr. Boyle; I said some things I didn't mean. I was just so surprised to see him here. You know? Did he tell you?

MRS BOYLE: No, Peter.

PETER: But I would do anything to get Rita back. *(Looking at the* OLD MAN*)* I love her with all my heart and soul...

MRS BOYLE: Well, she says that you're unstable and she's sorry she ever met you. I don't know, you don't seem so unstable to me.

PETER: No.

MRS BOYLE: Maybe I'm being naive.

PETER: No, you're not.

MRS BOYLE: That's what all unstable people say, Peter...I'm teasing you.

PETER: If I could just see her....

MRS BOYLE: You can't come here, Peter. If either of them knew I was talking to you, they'd have me shot at sunrise.

PETER: How's she been? Is she okay?

MRS BOYLE: Oh, I don't know what her problem is.

PETER: If she wants me to see a psychiatrist....

MRS BOYLE: Well...

(The OLD MAN *scribbles something on a pad and hands it to* PETER, *who reads as he talks.)*

PETER: Marion, what if...it's just a thought, but what if you told her I was going away on business for a couple of weeks —

MRS BOYLE: Are you?

PETER: No, wait.

MRS BOYLE: Oh.

PETER: And you said she could stop by to pick up the rest of her things from storage in the basement, you know, all her old letters and journals from her childhood and all that stuff she's left here, and then when you came by with her I'd be here. And we could talk.

MRS BOYLE: Oh, I don't know, Peter.

PETER: I have to see her. Even if she won't even speak to me... Please.

(Pause)

MRS BOYLE: When would you want us?

PETER: Anytime.

MRS BOYLE: I'm not promising anything.

PETER: I understand....

MRS BOYLE: Monday?

PETER: Monday's great.

MRS BOYLE: All right, I'll try. That's all I can do.

PETER: I understand. Thank you.

MRS BOYLE: What time?

PETER: Anytime.

MRS BOYLE: Noon, say?

PETER: Noon's great. Fine.

MRS BOYLE: High noon.

PETER: High noon.

MRS BOYLE: All right.

PETER: Thank you very much...

MRS BOYLE: Peter?

PETER: Yes?

MRS BOYLE: What you said before about Rita not being the same person?

PETER: Uh-huh?...

MRS BOYLE: They never are, Peter. They're never Rita. They're never Dr. Marshall Boyle, not the way that you think they should be. They're always someone else. They're always changing.

PETER: Uh-huh.

MRS BOYLE: That's life. That's marriage. They're always growing and shifting and so are you.

PETER: Right.

MRS BOYLE: She may not be the picture of the woman you thought she was, but that's an image, Peter. That's just a picture. Words.

PETER: I know.

MRS BOYLE: I'm sure you're not always the prize either.

PETER: No.

MRS BOYLE: Nobody is. But I know she loves you and misses you.

PETER: I miss her too.

MRS BOYLE: All right. We'll see you Monday then.

PETER: Thank you, Mom.

MRS BOYLE: All right.

PETER: Bye.

MRS BOYLE: Bye now.

(They both hang up. MRS BOYLE *disappears.)*

PETER: She'll try.

(Long pause. PETER *slowly kneels and kisses the* OLD MAN *tenderly on the mouth.)*

(The apartment. Darkness. RITA *and* MRS BOYLE *enter, switching on the lights.)*

MRS BOYLE: I don't want you to be angry with me.

RITA: I'm not. Relax.

MRS BOYLE: *(Looking around)* He keeps it clean.

*(*PETER *enters.* RITA *does not see him at first.)*

RITA: Yeah. He likes things in their proper— *(She sees* PETER.*)* —places.

MRS BOYLE: Now I want you to talk, Rita, I want you both to talk, that's all. Peter has something he wants to tell you. If after you've heard him out you don't want to stay, then I'll be downstairs in the car. You can do that much, since you took the trouble to marry him. You might actually thank me someday.

PETER: Mom, are you sure I can't get you something to drink?

MRS BOYLE: No, thank you, Peter. *(To* RITA*)* This was my idea, by the way.

*(*MRS BOYLE *goes out. Pause.)*

PETER: How've you been?

RITA: I'm sorry.

PETER: Why? You're here now.

RITA: I wanted to come, I just....

PETER: You did? Really? Well... It's been real lonely here without you, Rita. *(*PETER *has maneuvered into a position*

between RITA *and the exit. The* OLD MAN *appears behind*
RITA; *he carries a kitchen knife and a length of rope. She does*
not see him immediately.) You went to London, your
mom says. *(*RITA *turns, sees the* OLD MAN *as* PETER *grabs*
RITA *from behind.)* Okay. Tie his feet. *(*RITA *and the* OLD
MAN *are holding each other's gaze, unable to move.)* Rita!
Come on!

RITA: You don't have to do this.

PETER: Tie him!

*(*PETER *takes the rope as* RITA *and the* OLD MAN *continue to*
stare at one another.)

RITA: This is not necessary, kids.

PETER: Give me the knife. *(*PETER *still holds on to* RITA
from behind.) Give it to me! *(*PETER *takes the knife in one*
hand, holds RITA's *arm behind her back with the other.)*
Now kiss him. *(The* OLD MAN *kisses* RITA *on the mouth.*
They separate. PETER *releases* RITA *and wields the knife,*
particularly wary of the OLD MAN.*)* Rita?

OLD MAN: No. It didn't work.

PETER: *(To* RITA*)* Is it you?

*(*RITA *is shaking her head.)*

OLD MAN: No!

PETER: Rita?

RITA: I don't know how it happened. I don't know what
I did.

PETER: *(To* RITA*)* I'll kill you, I swear to god.

OLD MAN: Peter.

PETER: *(Threatening her with the knife)* How did you do
this? How the hell did you do this?

OLD MAN: Put the knife down, please.

PETER: *(To the* OLD MAN*)* I'll take care of this, Rita! It's a trick, don't you know that much?

OLD MAN: *(Overlapping)* He doesn't know. Give it to me. *(The* OLD MAN *is holding out his hand.)* Please. Peter.

*(*PETER *is looking from one to the other, paralyzed with doubt.)*

PETER: Are you here? Rita?

OLD MAN: I'm right here.

PETER: Talk to me if you're here.

OLD MAN: Give me the knife.

PETER: I can't. I'm sorry.

OLD MAN: Then just put it down. *(Slowly* PETER *lowers the knife.)* Thank you.

(Beat)

RITA: *(To the* OLD MAN*)* Where'd you go?

PETER: Watch him.

RITA: I couldn't imagine what happened to you.

OLD MAN: Twelve twenty-two Ocean Avenue.

RITA: How is Leah?

OLD MAN: I think she misses you.... She keeps putting on professional wrestling on the TV and I just sorta sit there, trying to look interested.

RITA: Interested? It's a joke. We laugh at it together.

OLD MAN: She keeps making soup and offering me another cup and another cup.

RITA: Oh, it's full of fat, she doesn't know how else to make it.... Your mother...she isn't serious about the peanut butter and mayonnaise?

OLD MAN: Oh, she made you one? A sandwich?

PETER: Stop this.

OLD MAN: I haven't had one of those since grade school, I forgot all about— Did you try it?

PETER: Rita!

OLD MAN: Oh, they're really good....

(Beat)

RITA: I wanted it, that's all. That's all I know. I'm not hiding anything from you; I don't know any more than that. I started out to take a walk. To just try and get as far away from me as I possibly could, I didn't care. I took the first bus I saw at Port Authority: "Englewood Cliffs". It sounded romantic enough.

OLD MAN: Englewood?

RITA: Yeah. I got off the first street corner; dogs came up to play. And what's this? A *wedding*. Young people starting a life. I had some champagne, nobody bothered me. What did it matter what I did? I wished to god I were that young bridegroom starting out. Or the bride, for that matter. Look at the shine in those eyes.

OLD MAN: You're kidding. I was freaked from the moment I woke up.

RITA: Yeah?

OLD MAN: I was terrified.

RITA: No, I thought to myself, If I could shine like the light of that girl over there, I'd never take another drink, I'd let my liver hang on another decade, stay out of the sun, eat right. This time I would floss.

OLD MAN: I remember now. It was you. Oh god, it was your eyes shining back. And you kissed me and, let me be over there, please, let me skip to the end of all this hard part. I wanted to be you. For one second of one day, what would it be like to just be. And—

RITA: Yes.

OLD MAN: —not be afraid.

(They begin to overlap one another ever so slightly.)

RITA: If I could just get inside.

OLD MAN: If I could get inside.

RITA: I'll kiss the bride. I'll be the bride.

OLD MAN: My whole life would be behind me.

RITA: My whole life would be ahead of me again. Look at her. The soft arms. The white teeth—

OLD MAN: That smell.

RITA: The sweet smell on her breath.

OLD MAN: A man.

RITA: Not like something rotting coming up from your insides, but soft—

OLD MAN: Like a father.

RITA: Like a baby. And white.

OLD MAN: An old man... With nothing—

(Together:)

OLD MAN/RITA: Nothing to lose. All you've got to do is want it. Bad enough.

(Their eyes are locked. The light in the room dims as if the sun outside were obscured by a cloud—a low rumble. RITA is now standing; the OLD MAN is now seated.)

RITA: My god.

OLD MAN: Like an old suit...

PETER: Rita?

OLD MAN: Don't you see? My wife and daughter had a bond. I loved them both so much I wanted to eat them alive.

RITA: I saw their photographs. Your mom. You just wanted them back, the way they were.

OLD MAN: And women cry, you think. It feels good.

RITA: Yes, it does.

OLD MAN: Women make a life inside their body and that life comes out and holds on to them—

RITA: Yes.

OLD MAN: Clings to them, calls them up from school and says, "I'm sick, Ma, come pick me up." That baby is theirs for life. Where are they now? My wife. My mother.

RITA: They're right here.

OLD MAN: To be able to look back from their side of the bed with their eyes. At last. *(To* PETER*)* And you, my boy. I tried to be patient, I tried to be interested. I called every hotel in Kingston, "What the hell is a Long Island Ice Tea?" You're a sweet kid, no hard feelings, but you're not my type....

PETER: Please.

OLD MAN: I don't know.... The idea of living forever... It's not so good. *(Beat)* And those parents of yours you can keep.

RITA: Thank you.

(The OLD MAN *walks to the door, turns back.)*

OLD MAN: Do yourselves a favor: Floss.

(He goes out.)

PETER: Rita?... Oh, Rita... Oh my beautiful...

RITA: My body. My body.

(He unties her feet.)

PETER: There they are. Look at those. Yes! Your hair.

RITA: I'm here. I'm not afraid.

PETER: I know.

RITA: I'm not afraid.

PETER: Oh, I love you…. Give me a smile. *(She does.)* Je hebt erg witte tanden. Je hebt erg witte tanden.

RITA: Ohhhhhh, I don't remember what I'm supposed to say, Peter, I know I memorized it.

PETER: Om je better mee op to eten.

RITA: You promised you'd tell me. What does it mean?

PETER: The better to eat you with. Oh, Ríta. Never to be squandered…the miracle of another human being.

RITA: You're the miracle.

PETER: No, you are.

RITA: You.

PETER: You.

(They clasp one another. Music plays. PETER lifts RITA and carries her, finally, across the threshold as the Vocalist sings: "How my lovesong gently cries/ For the tenderness within your eyes./My love is a prelude that never dies:/ My prelude to a kiss." Lights fade.)